FROM TADPOLE TO FROG

Anita Ganeri

www.heinemann.co.uk/library
Visit our website to find out more information about Heinemann Library books.

To order:
 Phone 44 (0) 1865 888066
 Send a fax to 44 (0) 1865 314091
 Visit the Heinemann Bookshop at www.heinemann.co.uk/library to browse
our catalogue and order online.

First published in Great Britain by Heinemann Library, Halley Court, Jordan Hill, Oxford OX2 8EJ, part of Harcourt Education. Heinemann is a registered trademark of Harcourt Education Ltd.

Editorial: Nancy Dickmann and Sarah Chappelow
Design: Ron Kamen and edesign
Picture Research: Ruth Blair and Kay Altwegg
Production: Helen McCreath

Originated by Modern Age
Printed and bound in China by South China Printing Company

13 digit ISBN 978 0 4310 5077 5 (HB)
10 digit ISBN 0 4310 5077 5 (HB)
10 09 08 07 06
10 9 8 7 6 5 4 3 2 1

13 digit ISBN 978 0 4310 5087 4 (PB)
10 digit ISBN 0 4310 5087 2 (PB)
11 10 09 08 07
10 9 8 7 6 5 4 3 2 1

The British Library Cataloguing in Publication Data
Ganeri, Anita
From tadpole to frog. - (How living things grow)
571.8'1789
A full catalogue record for this book is available from the British Library.

Acknowledgements
The Publishers would like to thank the following for permission to reproduce the following photographs:
Alamy p. 26; Ardea p. 5; Bruce Coleman p. 20 (Kim Taylor); Corbis pp. 6 (Anthony Cooper/Ecoscene), 8 (Jean Hall/Cordaiy Photo Library Ltd); FLPA pp. 9 (Wil Meinderts/Foto Natura), 11 (Alwyn J Roberts), 21 (Walter Rohdich), 22 (Derek Middleton), 23 (Rene Krekels/Foto Natura), 29 (John Tinning); Naturepl.com pp. 4 (William Osborn), 7 (Philippe Clement), 15 (Jurgen Freund); NHPA pp. 16 (Trevor McDonald), 17 (Stephen Dalton), 19 (Stephen Dalton), 24 (George Bernard), 25 (Stephen Dalton); Photolibrary.com pp. 10, 12, 13, 14, 27; Science Photo Library p. 18 (Dr Morley Read).

Cover photograph of a frog reproduced with permission of Corbis/Mary Ann McDonald.

Illustrations: Martin Sanders

Every effort has been made to contact copyright holders of any material reproduced in this book. Any omissions will be rectified in subsequent printings if notice is given to the publishers. The paper used to print this book comes from sustainable resources.

Contents

Words written in bold, **like this**, are explained in the glossary.

Have you ever seen a frog?

A frog is a kind of animal called an **amphibian**. They spend part of their lives in water and part on land. Frogs live all over the world.

This is a frog called a common frog.

Frogs spend most of their time in water.

You are going to learn about a common frog. You will learn how a frog is born, grows up, has babies, gets old, and dies. This is the frog's life cycle.

How does the frog's life cycle start?

5

Frogspawn

The frog starts life as a tiny egg in a pond. A **female** frog lays the eggs in spring. The eggs are called **frogspawn**.

The female lays hundreds of eggs at a time.

The eggs are covered in clear jelly. The jelly swells up in the water. This helps to keep the eggs safe.

The eggs stick together in a big ball.

What is in an egg?

Hatching eggs

Can you see the little black animal in each egg? Each one is a tadpole. The tadpole grows bigger and bigger in the egg.

This tiny tadpole will grow into a frog.

The eggs start to **hatch** after about 30 days. The tadpoles wriggle out of their jelly eggs.

Lots of eggs and tadpoles are eaten by frogs and birds.

Does the tadpole look like a frog?

Tiny tadpoles

The tadpole does not look like an adult frog. The tadpole has a long tail that she uses for swimming.

The tail makes the tadpole look like a little fish.

A frog cannot breathe underwater.
A tadpole can. The tadpole has
little slits called **gills**. The gills take
in air from the water for the tadpole
to breathe.

The tadpole eats her egg. Then she eats water plants.

How does the tadpole change into a frog?

Growing tadpoles

The tadpole grows bigger. Her body slowly starts to change. When she is about six weeks old, she grows two back legs.

The tadpole uses her back legs to swim faster.

Next, the tadpole grows **lungs**. She loses her **gills**. Now the tadpole has to swim to the **surface** to breathe in air.

The tadpole uses her lungs to breathe in air.

Legs and tails

About four weeks later, the tadpole grows two front legs. She now starts to look more like a frog.

*A tadpole's front legs grow through her **gills**.*

When the tadpole is twelve weeks old, her tail has almost gone.

The tadpole still uses her tail for swimming. But her tail is starting to shrink.

What is the tadpole called now?

15

Froglets

The tadpole now looks like a little frog. She is called a **froglet**. Her tail has gone.

She uses her back legs and feet for swimming.

The froglet starts to spend time out of the
pond. She climbs on to a leaf or a plant
by the water.

When does the froglet
leave the pond?

Life on land

The **froglet** is about four months old. She leaves the pond. She stays close to the water.

She hides among the long grass and stones.

She dives in to get her skin wet.

The froglet has to keep her skin damp. Her skin cannot dry out. She stays close to the water.

When is the froglet grown up?

Hungry frog

It takes the **froglet** about a year to grow up. Now she is called a frog. The frog eats **insects**. She catches them with her long, sticky tongue.

Animals like birds, bats, and grass snakes eat frogs. When the frog is in danger, she dives back into the pond.

This frog is in danger from a snake.

Where do frogs live?

Frogs at home

Adult frogs live in damp places on land. They live in gardens, meadows, and woods.

*Frogs go back to the pond to **breed**.*

A frog can live for about eight years if it does not get eaten.

Frogs often hide in the day. They hide from animals that might eat them. Frogs come out at night to look for food.

Where does the frog go in winter?

Winter sleep

In winter, it is cold. There is not much to eat. The frog goes into a deep sleep. This sleep is called **hibernation**.

The frog goes to sleep under a pile of leaves, moss, or stones.

Over winter, the frog's body slows right down to save energy. She wakes up in the spring when the weather is warmer.

Where does the frog meet a **mate**?

25

Meeting a mate

The frog is three years old. She is ready to **mate**. In spring, she goes back to the pond she was born in. She finds a **male** frog to mate with.

*Male frogs make a low, croaking sound to call the **females**.*

More books to read

Little Nippers: Life as a Frog, Vic Parker (Heinemann
   Library, 2003)

Life Cycles: Frog, Louise Spilsbury (Raintree, 2003)

Nature's Patterns: Animal Life Cycles, Anita Ganeri
   (Heinemann Library, 2005)

Websites to visit

Visit this website to find out more interesting facts
about frogs and their life cycle:

http://www.kiddyhouse.com/Themes/frogs/

Disclaimer

All the internet addresses (URLs) given in this book were valid at the time of going to
press. However, due to the dynamic nature of the internet, some addresses may have
changed, or sites may have ceased to exist since publication. While the author and
publishers regret any inconvenience this may cause readers, no responsibility for such
changes can be accepted by either the author(s) or the publishers.

Index